Editor
Stephanie Buehler, Psy.D.

Managing Editor
Ina Massler Levin, M.A.

Editor-in-Chief
Sharon Coan, M.S. Ed.

Illustrator
Ken Tunell

Cover Artist
Barb Lorseyedi

Art Director
CJae Froshay

Art Coordinator
Kevin Barnes

Imaging
James Edward Grace
Rosa C. See

Product Manager
Phil Garcia

Publisher
Mary D. Smith, M.S. Ed.

Vocabulary

GRADE 6

Author

Wanda Kelly

Teacher Created Resources, Inc.
6421 Industry Way
Westminster, CA 92683
www.teachercreated.com
ISBN-0-7439-3365-6
©*2003 Teacher Created Resources, Inc*
Reprinted, 2005
Made in U.S.A.

Table of Contents

Introduction

The old adage "practice makes perfect" can really hold true for your child and his or her education. The more your child has practice with and exposure to concepts being taught in school, the more success he or she is likely to find. For many parents, knowing how to help their children may be frustrating because the resources may not be readily available.

As a parent, it is also difficult to know where to focus your efforts so that the extra practice your child receives at home supports what he or she is learning in school.

Practice Makes Perfect: Vocabulary is designed to help practice word skills that are taught in the classroom. Vocabulary skills that are appropriate for grade six are presented in this book. The words that appear in this book are everyday vocabulary with some words chosen because of their association with specific school subjects: science, mathematics, and social studies.

Nearly all the words used appear on the Educational Developmental Laboratories (EDL) core vocabulary lists for the sixth grade. These are graded vocabulary lists researched by EDL and are the same lists textbook publishers use for their books.

The following standards or objectives will be met or reinforced as a student completes the practice pages in this book. These standards and objectives are similar to the ones required by your state and school district. In addition to being able to use a dictionary effectively, a sixth-grade student should be able to do the following:

- practice methods of increasing vocabulary
- recognize certain basic root words
- add prefixes and suffixes to root words
- use correctly words that have multiple definitions and uses
- classify and use words according to positive and negative connotations
- understand the vocabulary connected with their studies of science, mathematics, and social studies
- identify and use accurately homonyms, synonyms, and antonyms
- use correctly words that are similar in appearance but different in meaning
- interpret some common idioms
- classify words according to the way they sound
- compose couplets and write brief descriptions
- compare American and British English

Exercises are provided for the student to practice each skill. The section that includes idioms, euphonious words, and composing light verse is designed to generate interest in learning new words and to practice using words in different ways—to just have fun with words.

A short quiz appears at the end of each section, and the "Unit Assessment" at the end of the book reviews concepts covered throughout the book. The "Unit Assessment" is in a standardized test format so that the student can practice test-taking skills as well as the knowledge gained from the exercises.

Build Your Vocabulary

Improving your vocabulary will significantly increase your reading, writing, and listening skills. Here are some specific steps you can take to build your vocabulary:

1. **Practice trying to figure out the meaning of a word based on the way it is used.**

   Look at or listen to the other words that surround it for clues.

2. **Develop your own definitions for words.**

   First, check in the dictionary for pronunciations, definitions, and uses. Then, create your own definition, using words that you are already familiar with and can remember easily.

3. **Use the words you learn in your own writing and speaking.**

   A new word does not become fully a part of your vocabulary until you use it yourself. Make an effort to use any new words you read or hear—after you have done your dictionary research.

4. **Memorize the meanings of words.**

   You can do this by making up silly sentences or rhymes that will help you remember. Also, you can develop in your mind a picture or scene to help your memory.

5. **Use a thesaurus to find synonyms.**

   This can be useful when you want to avoid repeating the same word or want to use a more exact word than the one you first thought of. **Note:** There is a danger associated with the use of a thesaurus. The words listed do not have exactly the same meanings as the one you started with. It is necessary to use a dictionary along with a thesaurus to avoid the embarrassment that comes with using the wrong word.

6. **Read.**

   This is the single most important way to achieve a wider vocabulary. Of course, the best choices are books, magazines, and newspapers that are recommended by your teachers and parents because of their excellent content.

   But if you do not have such literature available on a rainy day, read a book you have already read before, making sure you can define every word according to the way it is used. This may seem rather boring, but your reading pleasure will increase as your vocabulary expands.

   Another possibility for those times when you are short on reading material is to read anything you can find. That includes cereal boxes, comic books, and the nursery rhymes and stories that were read to you when you were younger. New words can be found in many different places.

How Many Uses?

Many words from your daily conversation and writing can be used in a variety of ways. One example is the word *quarter:*

- Avery saves all his *quarters* in his largest piggy bank. (noun)

- A *quarter* portion of the estate was given to each of the four heirs. (adjective)

- *Quarter* the apple pie so that we can all have a piece. (verb)

Use each of these words two different ways. Refer to a dictionary to check the words' various definitions.

1. fast

   a. _____

   b. _____

2. side

   a. _____

   b. _____

3. number

   a. _____

   b. _____

4. good

   a. _____

   b. _____

5. just

   a. _____

   b. _____

6. retreat

   a. _____

   b. _____

Choose the Best Definitions

For each sentence below and on page 7, choose the definition that matches the way the italicized word is used in the sentence.

1. Senator Whistler took the *floor* to defend his position on the immigration bill.

    a. to knock down

    b. upper or uppermost surface

    c. right to address an assembly

2. Professor Watkins went to Australia to participate in the *dig*.

    a. an archaeological site

    b. to learn or discover

    c. to break up, turn over, or remove

3. My vigorous friend Audrey was a *rock* and stayed with me the entire time.

    a. move back and forth; zigzag

    b. stable, firm, dependable one

    c. naturally formed mineral

4. Attorney William Joseph's *opposite* in the case was Attorney Justine Modigliani.

    a. one that is contrary to another

    b. located directly behind or ahead of

    c. sharply contrasting

5. Catherine Laws, my sixth grade teacher, *holds* a degree in music also.

    a. to restrain; curb

    b. to have in one's possession

    c. to regard or consider

6. When we went sailing Saturday, the seas were very *heavy*.

    a. weighted down; burdened

    b. of great intensity

    c. violent, rough

7. The argument between the two wealthy adversaries quickly became *heated*.

    a. warm a building

    b. degree of warmth or hotness

    c. intense, as of emotion

8. The nomination committee decided to *block* the investigation of their decisions.

    a. to impede the passage of

    b. to support or strengthen

    c. to indicate broadly; sketch

Choose the Best Definitions *(cont.)*

9. The gardener was *broadcasting* grass seed on the football field.

    a. making known over a wide area

    b. sowing widely, especially by hand

    c. transmitting by air

10. One *feature* of the agreement was hotly debated in the House of Representatives.

    a. prominent article in a newspaper

    b. publicize or make outstanding

    c. distinctive quality or element

11. One requirement of the equestrian class is that you must *groom* your horse.

    a. to make neat and trim

    b. to clean and brush

    c. to coach or tutor

12. The official began to *hedge* when he was pressed for details.

    a. to enclose with hedges

    b. to protect against monetary loss

    c. to purposely make an indefinite statement

13. The two countries approved a *joint* agreement to regulate trade.

    a. formed by united action

    b. a place where two or more things are joined together

    c. a cut of meat for roasting

14. Mahoud stood on the shore and could do nothing as he watched the yacht *keel*.

    a. to fall as from fainting

    b. to capsize

    c. to lean to one side; tilt

15. A *local* custom was to meet at the general store to discuss the weekend's events.

    a. widespread; throughout the country

    b. pertaining to a particular place

    c. making many stops on a route

16. My parents began teaching us *moral* behavior when my brother and I were quite young.

    a. concerning the state of mind of a person

    b. conforming to established standards of good behavior

    c. teaching principles by stories or events

17. The townspeople found the actions of the newcomer *quaint*.

    a. unfamiliar or unusual

    b. delightfully pretty

    c. a trait or characteristic

Definitions Quiz

Find one match for each sentence.

1. Archie *floored* Mehitabel with his remarks.

    a. Mehitabel was stunned by Archie's remarks.
    b. Mehitabel was embarrassed by Archie's remarks.
    c. Archie made his remarks to Mehitabel from the second floor.

2. The statue of the soldier stood *opposite* the walkway to the courts building.

    a. The statue of the soldier stood in sharp contrast to the courts building.
    b. The statue of the soldier was placed in the walkway to the courts building.
    c. The statue of the soldier was across from the walkway to the courts building.

3. Station WXYZ's daily *broadcast* reaches millions of people around the world.

    a. Station WXYZ's daily transmission reaches millions of people around the world.
    b. Station WXYZ's daily e-mail reaches millions of people around the world.
    c. Station WXYZ's daily seed sowing reaches millions of people around the world.

4. After she caught him cheating, Mrs. Constable said that Abernathy had bad *morals*.

    a. Mrs. Constable said Abernathy did not appear cheerful.
    b. Mrs. Constable said Abernathy did not meet the standards of good behavior.
    c. Mrs. Constable said Abernathy did not read enough fables.

5. The visitor says that he thinks the village of Mendocino is *quaint*.

    a. The visitor finds the village of Mendocino cute.
    b. The visitor finds the village of Mendocino charming.
    c. The visitor finds the village of Mendocino attractive.

6. Last night the *feature* at the movie was about Alaskan wildlife.

    a. Last night the comedy at the movie was about Alaskan wildlife.
    b. Last night the story at the movie was about Alaskan wildlife.
    c. Last night the main film at the movie was about Alaskan wildlife.

7. Gus decided to *retreat* from the argument about who won the race.

    a. Gus decided to resolve the argument about who won the race.
    b. Gus decided to withdraw from the argument about who won the race.
    c. Gus decided to settle the argument about who won the race.

8. Prescott decided to attend the government class for *immigrants*.

    a. Prescott decided to attend the government class for those new to the country.
    b. Prescott decided to attend the government class for those leaving the country.
    c. Prescott decided to attend the government class for those who were planning to become ambassadors to the United Nations.

Add Prefixes to Change Meanings

These are some common prefixes and their meanings:

- *com/con*—with, together
  examples: *com*bine, *con*tract

- *em/en*—in, into
  examples: *em*ploy, *en*rage

- *im/in*—not, without
  examples: *im*polite, *in*sane

- *pre*—before
  examples: *pre*sume, *pre*vention

- *sub*—below
  examples: *sub*merge, *sub*versive

Use the prefixes above and the list below to "build" words. Write the definition of each word you build. Use each word below one time.

Example: polite

Word with Prefix: <u>*im*polite</u>   Definition: <u>not polite, discourteous</u>

| 1. pound | 3. occupy | 5. tribute | 7. form | 9. pose |
| 2. able | 4. proper | 6. marine | 8. mission | 10. valid |

Word with Prefix   **Definition**

1. _____   _____

2. _____   _____

3. _____   _____

4. _____   _____

5. _____   _____

6. _____   _____

7. _____   _____

8. _____   _____

9. _____   _____

10. _____   _____

Add Suffixes to Change Meanings

These are some common suffixes and their meanings.

to form nouns:

- *tion*—act of, state of, result of
  examples: reac*tion*, reflec*tion*

to form verbs:

- *ize*—to make, cause to become, resemble
  examples: author*ize*, sermon*ize*

to form adjectives

- *less*—deprived of, without, beyond the range of
  examples: defense*less*, harm*less*

Use the suffixes above and the list below to "build" words. Write the definition of each word you build. Use each word one time. Note that adding a suffix often affects the spelling of a word.

Example: care

Word with Suffix: *careless*   Definition: <u>inattentive, inconsiderate</u>

1. graduate	3. item	5. legal	7. product	9. seam
2. heed	4. personal	6. connect	8. price	10. relate

Word with Suffix   **Definition**

1. _____   _____

2. _____   _____

3. _____   _____

4. _____   _____

5. _____   _____

6. _____   _____

7. _____   _____

8. _____   _____

9. _____   _____

10. _____   _____

Prefixes and Suffixes Quiz

Select the correct word from the ones below to fill in the blanks in the sentences. (You may need to form plurals or add other endings to some words.)

seamless	improper	compound	enable	itemize
compose	production	graduation	priceless	preoccupy
personalize	conform	impose	commission	contribute

1. Annamarie, the clerk, was told that she would have to _____ every sale.

2. Even after he could not hear, Beethoven continued to _____ his music.

3. Because all the employees and company officers cooperated, the ABC Company and the XYZ Company were able to conduct a _____ merger.

4. The ABC Company continued its _____ of widgets.

5. Sebastian's parents were shocked by the _____ behavior exhibited by his friends.

6. The artwork that was hanging on the museum's walls was _____.

7. Receiving her college degree _____ Sybil to find a job teaching music in an elementary school.

8. If you are going to live in our house, you must _____ to the rules.

9. Maximillian decided not to _____ his problems by not doing his homework after he had done so poorly on his social studies test.

10. Everyone in my class was asked to _____ so that we could buy a gift for our teacher, Mr. Dunbar, who was ill.

11. Jervis was _____ to paint a portrait of President Worley.

12. For only one dollar more, I could have my backpack _____ with my initials.

13. Our whole family attended McKenzie's high school _____ ceremony.

14. Luana's mother did not want to _____ on anyone to pick her up after her car broke down in the mall parking lot.

15. It was difficult for Leann to sleep because she was so _____ with worry about her algebra test that she needed to study for.

Synonyms: Similar Meanings

Synonyms are especially important when you decide you need a more exact word or a better word to express your meaning when you are writing or reading. At such times, a thesaurus is a helpful reference.

Because a thesaurus entry usually contains several words that are considered synonyms, you need to also use a dictionary to be sure that the word you choose produces the meaning you want. You cannot be sure that every word in the list will work as a substitute for the one you started with.

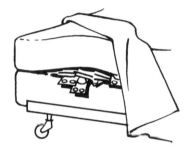

For example, you may want to describe in a story a character who is stingy, but you want a word that also suggests that the person hides away money. The thesaurus lists several words that could be used in place of *stingy*: *miserly, tightfisted, penny-pinching, cheap,* and *frugal*. One of these is the word you are looking for: *miserly*. When you look it up in the dictionary, you find that it means exactly what you had in mind: *being stingy and especially hiding money*.

Use a thesaurus and a dictionary to choose the best **synonyms** *to replace the italicized words in the following sentences. (Remember that one word often leads to another. You may have to go to the next step and look in the dictionary for definitions of one or more unfamiliar words in a definition.)*

---

1. The naturalized citizen, Maria Hernandez, pledged her *allegiance* to her new country.

   a. feasibility   b. helpfulness   c. loyalty

2. Without even a *whimper*, Baby Gerald let a complete stranger give him his bottle.

   a. whoopee   b. cry   c. twitch

3. Even the great Inspector Cleverleaux could not *unravel* the mystery.

   a. tighten   b. calculate   c. untangle

4. The neighbor's barking German shepherd, Daisy, interrupted my *slumber*.

   a. leisure   b. relaxation   c. sleep

5. Because he wanted to *qualify* to go to a top-notch university after he graduated from high school, Terence worked to earn excellent grades in all his classes.

   a. to be eligible   b. to be barred   c. to be innovative

6. Mozart wrote *operas* that are performed throughout the world.

   a. violin solos   b. plays set to music   c. plays about soaps

---

Synonyms: Similar Meanings *(cont.)*

7. Only an impolite and insensitive person will *mock* others.

     a. photograph   b. ridicule   c. impersonate

8. Molly thought she would *keel* over from exhaustion after running the marathon.

     a. collapse   b. recover   c. become ill

9. My friend Matthew is considered an *ideal* candidate for class president.

     a. indifferent   b. poor   c. perfect

10. The Burmese ruby and the Ceylon sapphire are both *gems* that Mrs. Trumpet likes.

     a. standouts   b. precious stones   c. gymnasium

11. It is *essential* that you eat healthful foods if you are going to remain healthy.

     a. extremely   b. indicated   c. necessary

12. I had to buy a new atlas because the *boundaries* of some countries changed.

     a. canopies   b. campaigns   c. borders

13. Mr. Chang, our new neighbor, is an *amateur* photographer.

     a. not expert   b. not formal   c. not effective

14. One of the events in speech contests in high school and college is *debate*.

     a. night crawlers   b. formal argument   c. bounty

15. My mother communicated to me an urgent *plea* to clean my room.

     a. pastime   b. query   c. request

16. It is always a bad idea to try to *deceive* your parents about anything.

     a. annoy   b. conceal   c. mislead

17. Sometimes it is difficult to decide what would be *suitable* to wear to an event.

     a. appropriate   b. considerate   c. communicate

Antonyms: Contrasting Meanings

Learning the antonym or the word that means almost the opposite of another word can help you better understand the meaning of that word just as a synonym can. Just as you may find exactly the right synonym in a thesaurus, you may also find an antonym in a thesaurus entry or in a dictionary. There are dictionaries that list both synonyms and antonyms.

Use a thesaurus and a dictionary to help you choose the sentence that best or most closely expresses the opposite meaning of the first sentence in each group. (Remember that one word often leads to another. You may have to go to the next step and look in the dictionary for definitions of one or more unfamiliar words in a definition.)

1. Pedro Herrera thought the salesman's smile was *artificial*.

    a. Pedro Herrera thought the smile was confident.

    b. Pedro Herrera thought the smile was sincere.

    c. Pedro Herrera thought the smile was amazing.

2. The very gracious Lord Hastings *ignored* Louisa's ink-smudged hands when she went through the reception line.

    a. Lord Hastings noticed Louisa's hands.

    b. Lord Hastings overlooked Louisa's hands.

    c. Lord Hastings admired Louisa's hands.

3. When visiting the sacred shrine, Murikama behaved very *respectfully*.

    a. Murikama was reverent at the shrine.

    b. Murikama was alert at the shrine.

    c. Murikama was irreverent at the shrine.

4. Mayor Lee is a *powerful* member of the city council.

    a. Mayor Lee is an insignificant member of the city council.

    b. Mayor Lee is a dedicated member of the city council.

    c. Mayor Lee is a distinguished member of the city council.

5. The Smokey Mountains are especially *gorgeous* in both the spring and fall.

    a. The Smokey Mountains are magnificent in spring and fall.

    b. The Smokey Mountains are ugly in spring and fall.

    c. The Smokey Mountains are amazing in spring and fall.

6. Bennie *warily* approached the wounded bear.

    a. Bennie cautiously approached the bear.

    b. Bennie recklessly approached the bear.

    c. Bennie unexpectedly approached the bear.

Antonyms: Contrasting Meanings *(cont.)*

7. The candidate *brooded* about the mistake he had made.

    a. The candidate worried about the mistake.

    b. The candidate took advantage of the mistake.

    c. The candidate was untroubled about the mistake.

8. Gracie was called a *heroine* after she foiled the robbery.

    a. Gracie was called a champion after the robbery.

    b. Gracie was called a coward after the robbery.

    c. Gracie was called a cadet after the robbery.

9. At the flea market, Luke found an *antique* vase for his mother.

    a. Luke found a very old vase at the flea market.

    b. Luke found a cunning vase at the flea market.

    c. Luke found a new vase at the flea market.

10. The senator appeared to be a very *dignified* person.

    a. The senator appeared to be very proper person.

    b. The senator appeared to he a very unseemly person.

    c. The senator appeared to be a very hideous person.

11. The house the astronomer lives in looks like a *palace* to me.

    a. The astronomer's house looks like a mansion.

    b. The astronomer's house looks like a hovel.

    c. The astronomer's house looks like a lobby.

12. Jo Ellen *concealed* the details of her illness from all of her friends.

    a. Jo Ellen revealed the details of her illness.

    b. Jo Ellen hid the details of her illness.

    c. Jo Ellen criticized the details of her illness.

13. Romeo decided that he would *forfeit* the race.

    a. Romeo decided that he would cultivate the race.

    b. Romeo decided that he would give up the race.

    c. Romeo decided that he would participate in the race.

14. Carl Sandburg wrote a *thorough* biography of Abraham Lincoln.

    a. Sandburg wrote a sketchy biography of Lincoln.

    b. Sandburg wrote a forlorn biography of Lincoln.

    c. Sandburg wrote a comprehensive biography of Lincoln.

Synonyms and Antonyms Quiz

*Match the **synonyms** or **antonyms** in the following lists of words.*

Synonyms

1. allegiance   _____   a. give up

2. itemize   _____   b. cautiously

3. forfeit   _____   c. formal argument

4. gem   _____   d. mislead

5. qualified   _____   e. eligible

6. dignified   _____   f. ridicule

7. debate   _____   g. loyalty

8. plea   _____   h. reverent

9. deceive   _____   i. precious stone

10. respectful   _____   j. list

11. mock   _____   k. proper

12. warily   _____   l. request

Antonyms

13. artificial   _____   m. revealed

14. amateur   _____   n. sincere

15. concealed   _____   o. expert

16. thorough   _____   p. sketchy

Synonyms and Antonyms Quiz _(cont.)_

Answer yes _or_ no _to each question._

1. Janelle was whimpering when she arrived home. _She was laughing._ Yes or no? _____

2. The detective unraveled the mystery. _He solved the mystery._ Yes or no? _____

3. The author's autobiography was thorough. _It was a detailed account._ Yes or no? _____

4. Because she owed Timothy a favor, Marcella felt obliged to contribute to the fund. _Marcella felt obligated to give to the fund._ Yes or no? _____

5. A suit is usually acceptable attire for a job interview. _A suit is usually inappropriate attire for a job interview._ Yes or no? _____

6. At their friend's birthday party, Josefina mocked Consuela. _Josefina ridiculed Consuela._ Yes or no? _____

7. The puppies were ideal companions for the sick child. _They were perfect companions for the sick child._ Yes or no? _____

8. Jason decided not to deceive his parents. _He decided to be truthful._ Yes or no? _____

9. The prizewinning photographer was an amateur. _The prizewinning photographer was a professional._ Yes or no? _____

10. Blackhawk is a distinguished leader of his tribe. _Blackhawk is a significant tribal leader._ Yes or no? _____

11. My mother allowed my slumber to continue until noon. _She let me sleep until noon._ Yes or no? _____

12. We detested the opera performance. _We enjoyed the violin solos._ Yes or no? _____

13. Mary and Jane debated about leaving. _They agreed to leave._ Yes or no? _____

14. Alexander was always able to conceal his emotions. _He was always able to reveal his emotions._ Yes or no? _____

Make the Right Choice

There are some words that are often used incorrectly. They are paired here because they are often used interchangeably, but they are completely different words and should not be substituted for one another.

For example, *reign* means to rule, and *rein* means to control or guide.

Correct: The king *reigned* for a very short time.

The rider tried to *rein* him in when the horse began to gallop.

Choose the correct words to complete the following sentences. You may need to refer to a dictionary.

1. **amount/number:** Lena and Chen could not figure out the
_____ of settings they would need for the banquet.

2. **beside/besides:** No one sat _____ me at the concert.

3. **continual/continuous:** The _____ chatter of the jays awoke me.

4. **council/counsel:** My father decided to _____ me about proper hygiene.

5. **farther/further:** How much _____ did you jog today?

6. **implied/inferred:** The policeman _____ that he thought that the man who
lives in the house down the street had committed the crime.

7. **principal/principle:** I was terrified when the _____ said she wanted to
see me in her office.

8. **advise/advice:** Was your counselor able to give you good _____ about
what you should do to solve your problem with Jocelyn?

9. **aisle/isle:** Teresa is ready to walk down the _____ and marry Ed.

10. **a lot/allot:** How much money did the committee _____ for publicity?

11. **can/may:** Joyce asked, "Mr. Jordan, _____ I leave the room?"

12. **later/latter:** Richard did not choose the former; he chose the _____
instead.

13. **moral/morale:** The speech Pat gave boosted my _____.

14. **Who's/Whose:** _____ going to make the pizza delivery to the haunted
house?

Clarify Expression

It is not always true that many words are needed to clearly express an idea. Sometimes an idea is expressed even better when fewer words are used and needless repetition is avoided.

Example: Mr. and Mrs. Creswell went to a <u>matinee performance</u> at the Roxy Theater.

Better: Mr. and Mrs. Creswell went to a <u>matinee</u> at the Roxy Theater. (The definition of *matinee is afternoon performance.*)

Rewrite the following sentences so that needless repetition is avoided.

1. The judge admonished the witness for trying to dance around the question.

   _____

2. Napoleon Bonaparte was small in stature.

   _____

3. Juda's plans were to fly to Puerto Rico by means of Pan American Airlines.

   _____

4. Elliott does not want to discuss the problem at this point in time.

   _____

5. One politician accused another of not revealing the real information in the bill.

   _____

6. The good items on the menu are in short supply.

   _____

7. I think he should have been removed from the position immediately.

   _____

8. Loretta used each and every excuse she could think of to avoid her daily chores.

   _____

9. For the obvious reason that he was wounded, the soldier called for a medic.

   _____

Use Specific Words

Both your writing and speaking will be improved if you carefully choose words that clearly express your ideas. Many times improvement can be achieved by substituting specific words for general ones.

> *Example:* Sidney <u>headed</u> to the finish line. (general)
> Sidney <u>*frantically raced*</u> to the finish line. (specific)

Substitute specific words for the italicized general words in the following sentences. (You may add modifiers for nouns and verbs.)

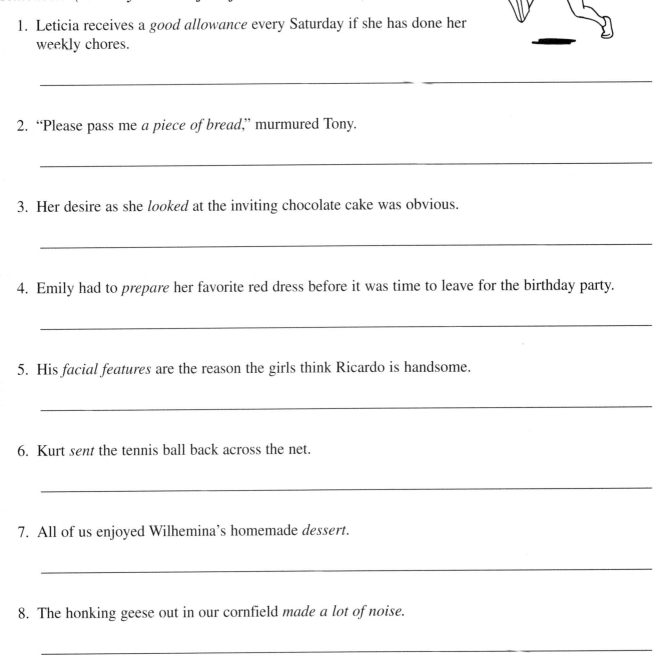

1. Leticia receives a *good allowance* every Saturday if she has done her weekly chores.

   _____

2. "Please pass me *a piece of bread*," murmured Tony.

   _____

3. Her desire as she *looked* at the inviting chocolate cake was obvious.

   _____

4. Emily had to *prepare* her favorite red dress before it was time to leave for the birthday party.

   _____

5. His *facial features* are the reason the girls think Ricardo is handsome.

   _____

6. Kurt *sent* the tennis ball back across the net.

   _____

7. All of us enjoyed Wilhemina's homemade *dessert*.

   _____

8. The honking geese out in our cornfield *made a lot of noise*.

   _____

Word Choice Quiz

*Label the sentence **C** if there are no word choice errors, or label it **I** if there are word choice errors. Where there are errors, write the correct choice on the line at the end of the sentence.*

_____ 1. Mr. Nichols asked how much farther we had to walk. _____

_____ 2. Bring that pink pillow besides you, please. _____

_____ 3. Mariko decided to a lot each person one cookie. _____

_____ 4. After I lost the race, my moral was low. _____

_____ 5. "What did Josie advise?" my mother asked. _____

_____ 6. "Cheating is against my principals," stated Jessica. _____

_____ 7. Whose the one who beat the seventh-grade girl in the race? _____

_____ 8. "May I help you?" the Robinson's clerk asked Father. _____

_____ 9. Yesterday the students all went to counciling sessions. _____

_____ 10. An embarrassed Leslie stumbled down the isle. _____

Choose one word in each sentence to make more specific. <u>Underline</u> the word you choose and then write the more specific word or words on the line. You may change and/or add words.

1. The happy youngster ran down the street. _____

2. Our neighbor's yard was covered with rubbish. _____

3. Johnny had on a new shirt. _____

4. He refused to eat the awful tasting salad. _____

5. The dog ventured into our backyard. _____

6. Rick's new motorcycle was black. _____

7. Donnie went to the movies. _____

8. Every morning my grandparents raise the flag. _____

Connotations and Synonyms

The dictionary defines *denotation* as the actual meaning of the word without any of the emotions we might attach to the word. However, there are many words that refuse to stay within the boundaries of denotation. They take on meanings that we may find very pleasing or that we may find very unpleasing. We call such emotional meanings of words *connotation*.

For example, would you rather be called *persistent* or *stubborn* or *pigheaded*? Generally, *persistent* is considered a neutral or favorable word. *Stubborn* is less favorable than *persistent*, but it is not as negative as *pigheaded*.

Therefore, of the three words, most of us would choose *persistent* to describe ourselves, *stubborn* to describe some of our friends or relatives when they cannot be persuaded to agree with us, and *pigheaded* to describe persons we often cannot seem to get along with very well.

In the groups of words below, rate each of the words or phrases. Label the word or phrase with the most neutral or favorable definition 1, the less favorable word or phrase 2, and the negative word or phrase 3. (You may need to refer to a dictionary.)

Example: pigheaded   ___3___

persistent   ___1___

stubborn   ___2___

1. thin _____ slender _____ skin and bones _____	4. candid _____ tactless _____ blunt _____
2. ugly _____ plain _____ unattractive _____	5. smug _____ satisfied _____ content _____
3. undersized _____ puny _____ petite _____	6. grave _____ unstable _____ critical _____

Denotation and Connotation Quiz

Label the following words **N** *if they have a negative connotation or* **P** *if they have a positive connotation. If a word meaning seems to be neutral, label it* **A.**

1. absurd   _____

2. weird   _____

3. reckless   _____

4. pulse   _____

5. monstrous   _____

6. devotion   _____

7. architect   _____

8. crisis   _____

9. agreeable   _____

10. despair   _____

11. icicle   _____

12. engage   _____

13. manicure   _____

14. poet   _____

15. tangerine   _____

16. utensil   _____

17. sag   _____

18. reform   _____

19. remote   _____

20. lanky   _____

21. wren   _____

22. solution   _____

23. respectful   _____

24. kerchief   _____

25. meddle   _____

26. fudge   _____

27. dungeon   _____

28. decay   _____

29. fake   _____

30. distinct   _____

31. frisky   _____

32. enrage   _____

33. lichen   _____

34. quiz (noun)   _____

35. snout   _____

36. vagabond   _____

37. sensible   _____

38. retort   _____

39. normal   _____

40. flourish   _____

Describe with Connotation

Write a description of a jungle animal. Use words with less favorable or negative connotations. (Be sure to keep your word choices within acceptable limits.) Give your description a title.

_____

_____

_____

_____

_____

_____

_____

_____

_____

_____

_____

_____

_____

_____

_____

_____

_____

_____

_____

Describe with Denotation

Using the same order, write another description of the jungle animal you wrote about for "Connotative Description" on the previous page. For this description, try to replace the connotative words with words that are neutral or without connotations. Give your description a title.

_____

_____

_____

_____

_____

_____

_____

_____

_____

_____

_____

_____

_____

_____

_____

_____

_____

_____

Helpful Prefixes

There are some commonly used prefixes that you will find helpful especially in your *science, mathematics,* and *social studies* schoolwork.

They will help you figure out and remember the meanings of words that you will find in your study of those subjects as well as in your general reading. In addition, you will use these words in other subjects, in everyday conversation, and in your writing.

anni/annu/enni—year   *dem/demo*—people   *mal/male*—bad, evil

chron—time   *ge/geo*—earth, soil, ground   *pend*—hang, weigh

circ/circum—around   *hydr/hydra/hydro*—water   *tra/trans*—across, through, over

List and define two words for each of the prefixes listed above. Try to choose words that you might expect to use in your study of science, mathematics and social science. On the third line, indicate the subject or subjects in which the word might be used (S, M, SS).

Example: dis   <u>disagreement</u>   <u>having different opinions</u>   <u>SS</u>

1. **anni/annu/enni**

   a. _____   _____   _____

   b. _____   _____   _____

2. **chron**

   a. _____   _____   _____

   b. _____   _____   _____

3. **circ/circum**

   a. _____   _____   _____

   b. _____   _____   _____

4. **dem/demo**

   a. _____   _____   _____

   b. _____   _____   _____

5. **ge/geo**

   a. _____   _____   _____

   b. _____   _____   _____

Helpful Prefixes *(cont.)*

6. **hydr/hydra/hydro**

   a. _____ _____ _____

   b. _____ _____ _____

7. **mal/male**

   a. _____ _____ _____

   b. _____ _____ _____

8. **pend**

   a. _____ _____ _____

   b. _____ _____ _____

9. **tra/trans**

   a. _____ _____ _____

   b. _____ _____ _____

Choose one word from each list to use in a sentence.

1. **anni/annu/enni:** _____

2. **chron:** _____

3. **cir/circum:** _____

4. **dem/demo:** _____

5. **ge/geo:** _____

6. **hydr/hydra/hydro:** _____

7. **mal/male:** _____

8. **pend:** _____

9. **tra/trans:** _____

Science Vocabulary

The following list contains words that are used in reading, writing, and speaking about science. Use them to fill in the blanks in the sentences below.

You may use each word only once.

acid	inherit	telescope
alloys	instinctively	tissues
antibiotic	nitrogen	tornado
barometer	predators	translucent
cell	prey	transparent
diverge	primitive	urban
enzyme	solar	vacuum
humidity		

1. When Lucas became ill, the doctor prescribed an _____.

2. Especially in the southern United States, people complain about the _____ in the summertime.

3. Our neighbors use _____ energy to heat their water.

4. The longer the twins were apart, the more their tastes began to _____.

5. Nickel is an element that is used in _____ and batteries, for example.

6. The baby will probably _____ his/her mother's curly hair.

7. An astronomer uses a _____ to study the galaxy.

8. The papaya contains an _____ that aids digestion.

9. Not everyone wants to live with the sounds found in an _____ environment.

10. Gazelles are often the _____ of lions and tigers.

11. _____ is often blamed for the digestive problems that people suffer.

Science Vocabulary (cont.)

12. The film that was put over the windows in our house was completely _____.

13. A _____ is the smallest structural unit of an organism that can function independently.

14. A _____ is a rotating column of air that can touch down on land and can leave tremendous devastation along its path.

15. A _____ is used to measure atmospheric pressure and is also used by meteorologists to help forecast the weather.

16. Those who study such things recommend that in order to be effective and to provide adequate light, lampshades should be _____.

17. Building nests, feeding their young, and teaching their young to fly is something that birds do _____.

18. _____ is a gaseous element that makes up nearly four-fifths of the air by volume.

19. Groups of cells that are similar in form and function are called _____.

20. A space that is relatively empty of matter is called a _____.

21. A person described as a _____ is one who belongs to a non-industrial society.

22. _____ such as lions and tigers chase, catch, and eat gazelles and other weaker animals.

Mathematics Vocabulary

Each line below consists of four words or terms. Three of the words in each line are words that may be used in reading, writing, and speaking about mathematics. Underline the one word in each line that does not fit with the other three.

1. gram   composite number   admission   align
2. bisect   bind   solid   multiplier
3. wave   gross   kilometer   decimal point
4. bar graph   trapezoid   percent   descend
5. hemisphere   divisibility   exponent   expedition
6. hygiene   circumference   bushel   calculate
7. square yard   vertical bar graph   lent   third power
8. axis   picket   radian   teaspoon
9. carat   inspect   quadrillion   acute triangle
10. octagon   isosceles triangle   mineral   liter
11. convention   horizontal   zero   median
12. maximal   fraction bar   pouch   metric system
13. mode   average   triangular prism   veil
14. picture graph   data   decameter   sulphur
15. decree   Fahrenheit   millimeter   centigrade
16. parallel planes cone   double-bar graph   chill
17. bracket   subtractive   prime factor   grave
18. migrate   semicircle   surface area   negative integer
19. cubic foot   decimal number   numb   line graph
20. estimation   gravity   combine   simpler form

Mathematics Vocabulary *(cont.)*

Write definitions for the following mathematics terms. (Be sure the definition you choose is the one for mathematics.)

1. gross _____

2. kilometer _____

3. hemisphere _____

4. bisect _____

5. radian _____

6. mode_____

7. meter _____

8. exponent_____

9. horizontal _____

10. circumference_____

11. gram _____

12. axis _____

13. solid _____

14. cone _____

15. percent _____

16. square _____

17. estimation_____

18. cube _____

19. bracket _____

20. semicircle_____

Social Studies Vocabulary

The following list contains words that are used in reading, writing, and speaking about social studies topics. Review them and look up the meanings of any you are not sure about.

abdicate	artifact	Buddhism	bureaucracy
Catholic	communism	democratic	Hinduism
humanitarian	linguist	literature	medieval
moral	myth	nationalism	naturalize
patronage	pope	Reformation	Renaissance
republican	socialism	stockbroker	vernacular

*Next, read the sentences below and on page 33. Choose the sentence from **a, b, or c** that most closely matches the numbered sentence.*

1. Maria was born in Mexico and last year became a naturalized citizen of the United States.

   a. Maria emigrated from Mexico to the United States where she studied the United States Constitution and eventually became a full-fledged citizen of the U. S.

   b. After she arrived in the United States, Maria appeared to become more natural.

   c. If you are born in Mexico, you can move to the United States and become a natural citizen.

2. Most of the developed countries of the world, including the United States, send humanitarian relief to the less developed countries that suffer from droughts and other natural disasters.

   a. Developed countries send humans to less developed countries.

   b. Less developed countries suffer from droughts caused by humanitarians.

   c. Developed countries send humanitarian relief to less developed countries.

3. Stockbrokers usually have backgrounds in economics, business, or a related field before they become agents who buy and sell stocks.

   a. Stockbrokers sell stocks in businesses that are economical.

   b. Stockbrokers are required to have degrees in economics or business.

   c. It is usual for stockbrokers to have studied economics or a related subject before they buy and sell stocks for others.

Social Studies Vocabulary *(cont.)*

4. Edward VIII was forced to abdicate the throne of England because he wanted to marry a woman who was a divorcée.

   a. Edward VIII had to choose between being king and marrying the woman who later became the Duchess of Windsor.

   b. Edward VIII had to give up the throne because he wanted a divorce.

   c. If a member of the British royal family wants to become a king a queen, then that person will have to get a divorce.

5. Democracy is government by the people where each person can be directly involved in the government or the people can elect representatives as the United States does.

   a. The United States does not have a democracy because of the United States Senate and the House of Representatives.

   b. The democracy in the United States is one in which the people elect representatives to form the government.

   c. The House of Representatives is part of a democratic government, but the Senate is not.

6. A republican government is one where the head of state is usually a president and the elected representatives of its people govern the country.

   a. The Republicans govern one half of the United States and the Democrats govern the other half.

   b. Both a democracy and a republic allow for representative government.

   c. In a republic, there is both an elected head of state, usually a president, and representatives elected by the people.

7. A linguist can often tell by listening to you speak what country or region of a country you are from or where you were living when you learned your language.

   a. The field of linguistics includes the study of various kinds of pastas, including linguini.

   b. A skilled linguist can listen to you speak and tell you whether you are from the northern or southern part of the state of Missouri.

   c. Once they begin studying linguistics, students are amazed to learn the various changes that have occurred in the English language.

8. Some people assert that the most important skill you can have in today's society is the ability to deal successfully with a bureaucracy.

   a. Bureaucrats are very skillful and very successful in today's society.

   b. The talent to be able to get what you want or need when you deal with a bureaucracy is valuable.

   c. Asserting themselves is a skill that bureaucrats develop very successfully.

Science, Mathematics, and Social Studies Quiz

Match the definitions with these words used in science, mathematics, and social studies.

1. antibiotic _____

2. mode _____

3. percent _____

4. barometer _____

5. humanitarian _____

6. linguist _____

7. octagon _____

8. instinctive _____

9. solar _____

10. hemisphere _____

11. alloy _____

12. naturalize _____

13. transparent _____

14. primitive _____

15. gross _____

16. republic _____

17. estimation _____

18. data _____

19. bureaucracy _____

20. abdicate _____

21. inherit _____

a. one part in a hundred

b. of a tribal culture

c. receive by genetic transmission

d. an eight-sided figure

e. mixture of two or more metals

f. administrative bureaus and departments

g. promoter of human welfare

h. approximate calculation

i. medicine

j. clear, sheer

k. most frequently occurring number in a distribution

l. formally relinquish power

m. an instrument that measures atmospheric pressure

n. half of a sphere

o. pertaining to the sun

p. factual information

q. expert in nature and structure of speech

r. head of state is president, not monarch

s. occurring naturally

t. twelve dozen; 144

u. grant full citizenship

Homonyms

Homonyms are two or more words that have the same sound and often have similar spellings, but they have *different meanings*. These words are problems for many writers, for it is easy to become confused by them.

If certain homonyms are a problem for you, you need to find a way to help you remember what each word means. For example, you can remember that *stationery* is writing paper because of the *er* in both station*er*y and pap*er*. Try to think of similar ways to distinguish one homonym from another so that you write both words correctly.

Select the correct homonyms to fill in the blanks in the sentences below.

1. Mrs. Ridley gave her _____ for all of us to watch the
   _____ of the colorful hot-air balloons as they rose over Albuquerque.
   (*ascent/assent*)

2. The sailors on the *Merry Mermaid* were trying to plot a safe _____
   (*coarse/course*) through the _____. (*straight/strait*)

3. The furniture refinisher did not want to use the _____ sandpaper. (*coarse/course*)

4. Just as important as remembering to give a _____ to someone else is
   having the ability to accept one gracefully. (*compliment/complement*)

5. Did you remember to _____ the references you used to write your
   report? (*cite/site*)

6. The climber kept the rope _____ as he made his way to the peak. (*taught/taut*)

7. If you look over _____, you will see _____ house
   that they have painted red, white, and blue. (*their/there*)

8. Learning your _____ (*well/will*) _____ (*lessen/lesson*)
   the chance that you will earn a poor grade.

9. Your _____ is required while I open my _____.
   (*presence/presents*)

10. Lucinda _____ the test, and that got her _____ the
    one thing that she had been dreading the most. (*passed/past*)

Idioms

An *idiom* is an expression that cannot be readily understood according to the actual meanings of the words in the expression. Instead, you have to hear the expression in a conversation that helps you figure out what it means. If you read the idiom, often the information that comes before and/or after the expression can help you figure out its meaning. Sometimes you have to ask someone else to help you understand an idiom.

No matter what language an idiom is in, if that language is not your first or native language, you will probably find it difficult to figure out what the idiom means. It can be humorous when someone who is not familiar with an idiom misinterprets it. Someone might think, for example, that your "mother had a cow" because you did not clean up your room.

Another problem that occurs with idioms is that some speakers and writers use them inaccurately, probably because they have never seen the idioms written and/or did not hear them clearly. That, too, can be humorous.

On the lines provided, write your translations of the following idioms:

1. We made it home safely, but it was *touch and go* there for awhile.

   _____

2. Jesse Morgan's boss told him to stop his *bellyaching*.

   _____

3. Yesterday we discovered our renters had moved out *lock, stock, and barrel.*

   _____

4. My mother said to my father, "*Simmer down.* Remember your blood pressure."

   _____

5. It doesn't take much for my brother to *get up on his high horse.*

   _____

6. Meredith was *as mad as a hornet* when she found out what had happened.

   _____

7. Winning the prize gave Richard *a big head.*

   _____

Euphoniously Speaking

Euphony describes a pleasing sound, especially words that are pleasing to the ear. Do you favor some words because of the way they sound? Do you dislike others because of the way they sound?

Euphony is a subject that interests poets and lexicographers (writers or compilers of dictionaries). A poet and lexicographer named Wilfred Funk (a euphonious name?) made a list of 10 words he considered the most beautiful words in the English language. The following words made Funk's list:

| chimes | luminous | dawn | melody | golden |
| mist | hush | murmuring | lullaby | tranquil |

Make a list of the 10 words that you consider the most beautiful words in the English language because of the way they sound to you when they are spoken. Listen to the rhythms of the syllables and to the sounds of individual letters as you "sing" aloud some of the words you are considering for your list. Try to avoid being influenced by the meanings and connotations of the words—not an easy thing to do.

_____   _____

_____   _____

_____   _____

_____   _____

_____   _____

Some teachers came up with a list of 10 words they consider harsh sounding or unpleasing words in the English language. The following words made their list:

| cough | grudge | crud | puce | flack |
| quark | gargoyle | screech | gawk | skink |

Use the same techniques you used to choose your most beautiful words to arrive at your list of the worst sounding words. Again, try to concentrate on the words' sounds and not their meanings. It might help to have someone else speak or sing the words on your list of possibilities before you make your final choice.

_____   _____

_____   _____

_____   _____

_____   _____

A Little Light Verse

Some famous poets are noted for their light verse; for example, Lewis Carroll, Ogden Nash, and Edward Lear all wrote whimsical poems. They had fun rhyming unusual or made-up words for their poems.

These are two lines from Lewis Carroll's "Jabberwocky":

'Twas brillig and the slithy toves did gyre and gimble in the wabe,

All mimsy were the borograves and the mome raths outgrabe."

- *Below are some pairs of rhyming words that you may use at the ends of the lines when you compose your own light verse, or you may make up your own.*

- *After you have written five or more couplets (two lines of rhythmic, rhyming verse), put them together to make one long poem.*

- *You may put the couplets in any order you wish to make your longer poem, and you may then decide you want to make some changes to perfect your poem.*

- *Give your poem a title.*

Rhythm: You may use the same rhythm Carroll used, the one used in one of your favorite poems, or develop your own. (Tap out the rhythm of each line as you read it aloud.)

Rhymes:

jimbley	bisky	drina	vernum	arkla	libbles
mimbley	tisky	trina	jernum	larkla	gribbles

1. _____

_____

2. _____

_____

3. _____

_____

4. _____

_____

5. _____

_____

Word Pictures

Try to "draw" a picture with words by describing the scenes or situations listed below. Use your imagination and as few words as possible, but write complete sentences.

Example: four people laying cards.

Word Picture: The four players sat at the card table, each carefully arranging her cards while she sneaked glances at the other three. *(or)* When I walked into the room, all four of the five-year-olds were yelling as loudly as they could, "Go Fish!"

1. a flock of geese flying south for the winter

   _____

   _____

2. two youngsters building a snowman

   _____

   _____

3. an elderly man or woman planting a garden

   _____

   _____

4. a group of ladies having lunch together in a restaurant

   _____

   _____

5. a class of preschool children walking to the park

   _____

   _____

5. a dog that wants to go for a walk

   _____

   _____

American and British English

Though many Americans brought their language with them from Britain, changes have occurred over the years. As a result, there are some things for which the two groups have different labels.

Match each Briticism with its American equal. Write your answer on the line provided.

British	American	
1. lift	a. napkin	_____
2. underground	b. sofa	_____
3. telly	c. hood (of a car)	_____
4. barmy	d. truck	_____
5. chips	e. guy	_____
6. redundant	f. elevator	_____
7. settee	g. druggist	_____
8. petrol	h. TV	_____
9. bloke	i. police officer, cop	_____
10. bobby	j. run (in a stocking)	_____
11. lorry	k. subway	_____
12. chemist	l. crazy	_____
13. ring up	m. call up	_____
14. mackintosh	n. gasoline	_____
15. serviette	o. raincoat	_____
16. pub	p. French fries	_____
17. sweet-shop	q. bar	_____
18. ladder	r. laid off	_____
19. bonnet	s. candy store	_____
20. starkers	t. naked	_____

Unit Assessment

Choose from **a, b,** *and* **c** *the word that means almost the same as the numbered word. Fill in the bubble.*

1. absurd
   - (a) serious
   - (b) ridiculous
   - (c) modest

2. antibiotic
   - (a) medicine
   - (b) capsule
   - (c) syrup

3. hedge
   - (a) tree
   - (b) hide
   - (c) evade

4. quaint
   - (a) remote
   - (b) foreign
   - (c) strange

5. retreat
   - (a) leave
   - (b) conference
   - (c) lake

6. impolite
   - (a) discourteous
   - (b) politics
   - (c) poultice

7. submerge
   - (a) kneel
   - (b) sink
   - (c) hover

8. inconsiderate
   - (a) defenseless
   - (b) unfair
   - (c) thoughtless

9. commission
   - (a) origination
   - (b) assignment
   - (c) church

10. allegiance
    - (a) declare
    - (b) allege
    - (c) loyalty

11. slumber
    - (a) wood
    - (b) yellow
    - (c) sleep

12. essential
    - (a) necessary
    - (b) request
    - (c) appropriate

13. mislead
    - (a) weapon
    - (b) unhappy
    - (c) deceive

14. artificial
    - (a) fake
    - (b) sincere
    - (c) disguised

15. warily
    - (a) cautiously
    - (b) heavily
    - (c) recklessly

16. dignified
    - (a) elderly
    - (b) proper
    - (c) intelligent

Unit Assessment (cont.)

17. plea
    (a) consent
    (b) request
    (c) speed

18. whimpering
    (a) seeking
    (b) crying
    (c) yelping

19. acceptable
    (a) suitable
    (b) appreciable
    (c) lamentable

20. counsel
    (a) meeting
    (b) committee
    (c) advise

21. candid
    (a) honest
    (b) deceitful
    (c) thorough

22. transparent
    (a) clear
    (b) hazy
    (c) window

23. diverge
    (a) challenge
    (b) swerve
    (c) converge

24. instinctively
    (a) confidently
    (b) naturally
    (c) hurriedly

25. bisect
    (a) cult
    (b) reduce
    (c) cut in half

26. gross
    (a) 154
    (b) 12 dozen
    (c) 3 dozen

27. horizontal
    (a) flat
    (b) vertical
    (c) typical

28. moral
    (a) dishonest
    (b) principled
    (c) confident

29. artifact
    (a) bowl
    (b) scalp
    (c) relic

30. data
    (a) information
    (b) graph
    (c) atlas

31. strait
    (a) winding
    (b) passage
    (c) honest

32. complement
    (a) addition
    (b) praise
    (c) balance

33. hydroplane
    (a) water-skimming boat
    (b) watery plain
    (c) a pressure point

34. frisky
    (a) chancy
    (b) playful
    (c) lanky

Unit Assessment *(cont.)*

Choose from **a, b,** *and* **c** *the word that means almost the opposite of the numbered word.*

1. devotion
   - (a) worship
   - (b) disloyalty
   - (c) dedication

2. despair
   - (a) misery
   - (b) two
   - (c) joy

3. improper
   - (a) inappropriate
   - (b) suitable
   - (c) laudable

4. unravel
   - (a) tangle
   - (b) yarn
   - (c) dance

5. ignore
   - (a) overlook
   - (b) notice
   - (c) meander

6. reverent
   - (a) disrespectful
   - (b) admiring
   - (c) reverse

7. brooding
   - (a) celebrating
   - (b) worrying
   - (c) languishing

8. forfeit
   - (a) surrender
   - (b) lose
   - (c) retain

9. amateur
   - (a) professional
   - (b) local
   - (c) novice

10. artificial
    - (a) synthetic
    - (b) natural
    - (c) planted

11. qualified
    - (a) eligible
    - (b) failed
    - (c) piqued

12. ideal
    - (a) thought
    - (b) wrong
    - (c) perfect

13. admonish
    - (a) reprimand
    - (b) approve
    - (c) propel

14. puny
    - (a) awesome
    - (b) weak
    - (c) strong

15. prey
    - (a) predator
    - (b) prayerful
    - (c) animal

16. meddle
    - (a) disregard
    - (b) metal
    - (c) center

Unit Assessment *(cont.)*

Choose from **a**, **b**, *and* **c** *the definition of the numbered word.*

1. circumference
   - (a) boundary line of a circle
   - (b) measurement of land area equal to 4,840 square yards
   - (c) unit of weight for precious stones

2. bracket
   - (a) a clear watery fluid
   - (b) one of a pair of marks to enclose written material
   - (c) having a sharp, acrid taste or smell

3. linguist
   - (a) specialist in nature and structure of speech
   - (b) one who loves, supports, and defends his country
   - (c) a man who is active in sports

4. stockbroker
   - (a) cowboy who tames horses
   - (b) professional who breaks up conglomerates
   - (c) agent who buys and sells stocks

5. abdicate
   - (a) betray one's country
   - (b) dictate the rules of the game
   - (c) formally relinquish power

6. vernacular
   - (a) small animals such as rats
   - (b) standard native language of country or locality
   - (c) occurring in the spring

7. percent
   - (a) intersecting at or forming right angles
   - (b) being remorseful
   - (c) out of each hundred; per hundred

8. dungeon
   - (a) a dark, often underground prison cell
   - (b) a short, heavy club
   - (c) a place frequented by people for relaxation

9. vagabond

    (a) person without a permanent home; wanderer

    (b) person who flees in search of shelter; refugee

    (c) person who is a representative for a cause; spokesman

10. local

    (a) occurring beneath the surface of the earth

    (b) occurring widely

    (c) pertaining to a particular place; not widespread

11. broadcast

    (a) to make known over a wide area

    (b) to make plain and clear

    (c) to turn or direct

12. presume

    (a) to make ready

    (b) to bear down on

    (c) to take for granted

13. seamless

    (a) without a break across the surface

    (b) made or used for ocean voyages

    (c) a woman who sews as an occupation

14. mock

    (a) a gray and white songbird

    (b) to make a full-sized scale model

    (c) to mimic with derision

15. gorgeous

    (a) especially beautiful

    (b) covered with gore; bloody

    (c) pleasing characteristic or quality

16. imply

    (a) to conclude from evidence or premises

    (b) to express or indicate indirectly

    (c) to yield to

17. stature

    (a) natural height in an upright position

    (b) sculptured likeness

    (c) law enacted by a legislature

Answer Key

How Many Uses? page 5

Answers will vary. Examples:

1. Avery's *fast* lasted six days. (n)
   My new watch is *fast*. (adj)
2. Avery stood by his friend's *side*. (n)
   The thief left by the *side* door. (adj)
3. Which *number* did you draw? (n)
   Number your paper one through six. (v)
4. Get a *good* night's sleep before the test. (adj)
   The peddler sold his *goods* from a truck. (n)
5. Our lawyer thinks we have a *just* cause. (adj)
   That cake has *just* enough chocolate in it. (adv)
6. Our captain ordered a *retreat* from the field. (n)
   "*Retreat*!" yelled our captain. (v)

Choose the Best Definitions, pages 6 & 7

1. c
2. a
3. b
4. a
5. b
6. c
7. c
8. a
9. b
10. c
11. b
12. c
13. a
14. c
15. b
16. b
17. a

Definitions Quiz, page 8

1. a
2. c
3. a
4. b
5. b
6. c
7. b
8. a

Add Prefixes to Change Meanings, page 9

Definitions will vary.
Possible definitions:

1. *com*pound—to combine, mix
2. *en*able—make able
3. *pre*occupy— to occupy completely the attention of
4. *im*proper—not suitable
5. *con*tribute—to give a share to

6. *sub*marine—a ship capable of operating under water
7. *con*form—to be in agreement; *in*form—to give information to
8. *com*mission—authority to carry out a task; *sub*mission—yielding to authority of another
9. *com*pose—to make up; *im*pose—to force on others
10. *in*valid—not justified

Add Suffixes to Change Meanings, page 10

Definitions will vary.
Possible definitions:

1. gradua*tion*—commencement ceremony
2. heed*less*—not pay attention to
3. item*ize*—to list
4. personal*ize*—to have printed with one's name
5. legal*ize*—permitted by law
6. connec*tion*—union, junction, link
7. produc*tion*—output
8. price*less*—invaluable
9. seam*less*—without a wrinkle or crack
10. rela*tion*—connection by blood or marriage; kinship

Prefixes and Suffixes Quiz, page 11

1. itemize
2. compose
3. seamless
4. production
5. improper
6. priceless
7. enabled
8. conform
9. compound
10. contribute
11. commissioned
12. personalized
13. graduation
14. impose
15. preoccupied

Synonyms: Similar Meanings, pages 12 and 13

1. c
2. b
3. c
4. c
5. a
6. b
7. b
8. a
9. c
10. b
11. c
12 c
13. a
14. b
15. c
16. c
17. a

Antonyms: Contrasting Meanings, pages 14 and 15

1. b
2. a
3. c
4. a
5. b
6. b
7. c
8. b
9. c
10. b
11. b
12. a
13. c
14. a

Synonyms and Antonyms Quiz, pages 16 and 17

Synonyms

1. g
2. j
3. a
4. i
5. e
6. k
7. c
8. l
9. d
10. h
11. f
12. b

Antonyms

13. n
14. o
15. m
16. p

page 17

1. no
2. yes
3. yes
4. yes
5. no
6. yes
7. yes
8. yes
9. no
10. yes
11. yes
12. no
13. no
14. no

Answer Key (cont.)

Make the Right Choice, page 18

1. number
2. beside
3. continuous
4. counsel
5. farther
6. implied
7. principal
8. advice
9. aisle
10. allot
11. may
12. latter
13. morale
14. Who's

Clarify Expression, page 19

Answers may vary. Examples:

1. ...for avoiding the question.
2. ...was short.
3. ...fly to Puerto Rico on Pan American Airlines.
4. ...the problem now.
5. ...not revealing the bill's contents.
6. ...are few.
7. ...should have been fired *or* demoted *or* removed.
8. ...used every excuse... .
9. Because he was wounded, ...

Use Specific Words, page 20

Answers will vary. Examples:

1. five dollars
2. a sourdough roll
3. stared greedily
4. wash and press
5. dreamy brown eyes and high cheekbones
6. smashed
7. apple strudel
8. sounded like a pack of barking dogs

Word Choice Quiz, page 21

1. C
2. I—beside
3. I—allot
4. I—morale
5. C
6. I—principles
7. I—Who's
8. C
9. I—counseling
10. I—aisle

Answers will vary. Examples:

1. The happy youngster ran down <u>Sixth Avenue</u>.
2. Our neighbor's yard was covered with <u>cans and old magazines</u>.

3. Johnny had on a new <u>neon green T-shirt</u>.
4. He refused to eat the <u>sour potato</u> salad.
5. The <u>brown Labrador</u> ventured into our backyard.
6. Rick's new <u>classic Harley</u> was black.
7. Donnie went to see <u>Lord of the Rings</u>.
8. Every morning my grandparents raise the <u>Stars and Stripes</u>.

Connotations and Synonyms, page 22

1. thin—2 slender—1 skin and bones—3
2. ugly—3 plain—1 unattractive—2
3. undersized—2 puny—3 petite—1
4. candid—1 tactless—3 blunt—2
5. smug—3 satisfied—2 content—1
6. grave—3 unstable—1 critical—2

Denotation and Connotation Quiz, page 23

Note: Some words acquire different connotative shades in different contexts. For example, "He fought the evildoer with <u>reckless</u> abandon," versus "He drove through the schoolyard of children with <u>reckless</u> abandon." Ask the student to explain or illustrate how the word shows a positive or negative connotation.

1. N		21. A	
2. N		22. P	
3. N		23. P	
4. A		24. A	
5. N		25. N	
6. P		26. A	
7. A		27. N	
8. A		28. N	
9. P		29. N	
10. N		30. A	
11. A		31. P	
12. P		32. N	
13. P		33. A	
14. A		34. A	
15. A		35. N	
16. A		36. A	
17. N		37. P	
18. P		38. A	
19. N		39. P	
20. A		40. P	

Science Vocabulary, pages 28 and 29

1. antibiotic
2. humidity
3. solar
4. diverge
5. alloys
6. inherit
7. telescope
8. enzyme
9. urban
10. prey
11. Acid

12. transparent
13. cell
14. tornado
15. barometer
16. translucent
17. instinctively
18. Nitrogen
19. tissues
20. vacuum
21. primitive
22. Predators

Mathematics Vocabulary, pages 30 and 31

1. admission
2. bind
3. wave
4. descend
5. expedition
6. hygiene
7. lent
8. picket
9. inspect
10. mineral
11. convention
12. pouch
13. veil
14. sulphur
15. decree
16. chill
17. grave
18. migrate
19. numb
20. gravity

1. total of 144 items; 12 dozen
2. metric measurement equal to 0.62 of a mile
3. half of a sphere
4. to cut or divide into two parts
5. a unit of angular measure equal to approximately 57° 17' 44.6"
6. the number in a distribution that occurs the most frequently
7. metric measurement equal to 3.28 feet or 1.09 yards
8. number or symbol placed to the right of and above another number denoting the power to which it is to be raised
9. at right angles to a vertical line
10. the boundary line of a circle
11. metric measurement equal to 0.035 of an ounce
12. a center line to which part of a structure or body may be referred
13. a geometric figure having three dimensions
14. surface generated by a straight line passing through a fixed point and moving along a fixed curve

Answer Key *(cont.)*

Mathematics Vocabulary, pages 30 and 31 *(cont.)*

15. one part in a hundred
16. the product of a number or quantity multiplied by itself
17. a rough calculation
18. the third power of a number or quantity
19. one of a pair of marks used to enclose written or printed material
20. half of a circle as divided by a diameter

Social Studies Vocabulary, pages 32 and 33

1. a
2. c
3. c
4. a
5. b
6. c
7. b
8. b

Science, Mathematics, and Social Studies Quiz, page 34

1. i
2. k
3. a
4. m
5. g
6. q
7. d
8. s
9. o
10. n
11. e
12. u
13. j
14. b
15. t
16. r
17. h
18. p
19. f
20. l
21. c

Homonyms, page 35

1. assent, ascent
2. course, strait
3. coarse
4. compliment
5. cite
6. taut
7. there, their
8. lesson, lessen
9. presence, presents
10. passed, past

Idioms, page 36

Answers will vary. Examples:

1. uncertain
2. complaining
3. completely
4. Calm down.
5. become offended
6. very angry
7. made Richard egotistical

American and British English, page 40

1. f
2. k
3. h
4. l
5. p
6. r
7. b
8. n
9. e
10. i
11. d
12. g
13. m
14. o
15. a
16. q
17. s
18. j
19. c
20. t

Unit Assessment, pages 41 and 42

1. b
2. a
3. c
4. c
5. a
6. a
7. b
8. c
9. b
10. c
11. c
12. a
13. c
14. a
15. a
16. b
17. b
18. b
19. a
20. c
21. a
22. a
23. b
24. b
25. c
26. b
27. a
28. b
29. c
30. a
31. b
32. c
33. a
34. b

Page 43

1. b
2. c
3. b
4. a
5. b
6. a
7. a
8. c
9. a
10. b
11. b
12. b
13. b
14. c
15. a
16. a

Pages 44 and 45

1. a
2. b
3. a
4. c
5. c
6. b
7. c
8. a
9. a
10. c
11. a
12. c
13. a
14. c
15. a
16. b
17. a